There Was and How Much There Was

Zeina Hashem Beck

smith|doorstop

Published 2016 by
smith|doorstop Books
The Poetry Business
Bank Street Arts
32-40 Bank Street
Sheffield S1 2DS

Copyright © Zeina Hashem Beck 2016
All Rights Reserved

ISBN 978-1-910367-71-1

Designed and Typeset by Utter
Printed by Biddles Books

Acknowledgements

Thanks to the editors of the following publications, in which some of these poems first appeared, sometimes in earlier versions, or are forthcoming: *Ambit*, *At Length*, *The Clearing*, *HeArt*, *The High Window*, *Literary Mama*, *Magma*, *One*, *World Literature Today* and the anthology *Red Sky: poetry on the global epidemic of violence against women*.

smith|doorstop Books are a member of Inpress: www.inpressbooks.co.uk. Distributed by Central Books Ltd., 99 Wallis Road, London E9 5LN

The Poetry Business gratefully acknowledges the support of Arts Council England.

Contents

5	Layla
6	Mother, Three Portraits
	1. Portrait of Mother as Jane Fone-da
	2. Portrait of Mother with Cigarette
	3. Portrait of Mother with Washing Machine
9	Untouched
10	Hiyam
11	Sestina: Gardenias
13	She Means It
14	Shoulders
15	Why I Hate Silent Movies
16	Recipes
18	Mother, Ka'aba
19	Milk
20	Room 607
21	The Invented Mothers
22	Fatimah (The Mother Of Her Father)
23	Say Love Say God
25	There Was and How Much There Was
32	Notes

For Mom – her stories,
For my daughters – their questions,
For Marwan – always,
For my girlfriends – our laughter,
For women everywhere – you are goddesses

Layla

I am tired of the love poems Qays keeps
tracing for me in the sand. What a luxury,
to roam mad with love, be punished only
with a tender name – *Majnun*. The world will always
forgive the foolishness of men. I'm the one who endures
the weight of another in the night. I remind myself
to cup my breasts and say they are mine. My thighs
mine, mine. Sometimes I tell him no, not tonight,
I'm bleeding again, and he believes me.
It's easy to believe anything about a body
that splits itself open and survives,
produces milk the next day. If I keep still
long enough, I hear the music inside
my veins; it sounds like women, singing.

Mother, Three Portraits

1. Portrait of Mother as Jane Fone-da

And she dressed for it too –
the headband, the leotard, the leg
warmers, the sneakers. All color-
coordinated. I sat on the table, moved
to the side for this daily ritual, pushed
the full ashtray away, listened
to the breathing that seemed
all exhale, exhale.

It was a kind of prayer, this twitching
of biceps and triceps, this body –
left, right, left
in the middle of our living room.

They were both blonde, both slim,
but Mom always sweat more,
said *if only, if only*,
that she could have done much
better than this "Jane Fone-da."

2. Portrait of Mother with Cigarette

Sometimes I woke
to the sound of her lighter,

small yet making its way
through the night.

I knew the only
visible thing in the dark

living room was the red end
of her Marlboro,

burning
with a faint paper sound,

retreating into itself.

3. Portrait of Mother with Washing Machine

I don't ask her why she is crying.
She lights a cigarette, talks about the hours

spent slicing the skins of olives
on the balcony, in the sun.

She says in her dream, she always
pulls out her two front teeth.

(I imagine the wound
where the roots throbbed.)

Oh how she wants to hold on
to a whale's fin, plough

an entire ocean on its back.
Or drive her car beyond

the streets of this small town.
But the clothes, they are stuck

in the washing machine.
When I tell her the electricity

would be back soon, she says,
Don't name your daughter after me.

Untouched

Years later, Mom would explain –
my aunt just wanted to give "that dog"
a scare. I wasn't sure whether she meant
the husband or the father.
My aunt had swallowed rat poison,
thinking she would dive and emerge
on one side or the other. She somehow
managed to emerge on both. (I can still see her
in our corridor, smiling. All teeth
and short curly hair, like a poodle.)
I don't know who found her, don't dare
ask, take in only what Mom mentions.

Like how my aunt woke up
from her coma one day,
hungry, dying to see
her little boys. How Mom left the house
with a bar of soap (square, wrapped
in brown paper) and a shampoo bottle,
saying she was going to clean
her little sister up. I remember her back
with the soap and shampoo

untouched, declaring she was happy
her sister had woken up for a day.
Because this meant she hadn't
killed herself, her death was merely
a doctor's mistake, she would surely
be allowed into heaven.

Hiyam

My grandmother, Hiyam, whose name
means love, had none, gave none. Locked
her refrigerator door so her children wouldn't
make a mess in the kitchen, sat them down,
fed them their sandwiches bite by bite until
they got bored and said they were full. Brushed
the tassels hanging from the sofa. Cleaned
the faucets until they shone
like silver flamingo necks. Beat anyone
who sat on the beds after they were made. Forgave
no one, not even her own skin. Drowned
herself a little more each day in the lake
of her mirror, dropped a pill, two pills, ten pills
in each morning – *goodbye, goodbye,*
most beautiful girl in Damascus. Retreated
when she noticed the wrinkles around her eyes –
first to the sofa, then into her bedroom, then into

her own mind. A week ago, she crouched
next to her bed, screamed at the shadows
to leave her alone, told them
she didn't want to eat chicken,
promised her dead son she would tell everyone
he said hello, took off her clothes, accused
her husband of stealing her new skirt,
the one she had bought
twenty-something years ago – Where is it, she asked,
Why, you fool, did you take it away?
Calmed down when Mom arrived and told her
she'd taken the skirt to iron it, would bring it back
tomorrow. Went out on the balcony
for the first time in years, looked outside,
I know this thing. It's called a street.

Sestina: Gardenias

The whiskey tears puddle behind your eyes.
This morning you think of suicide again,
but not really. Every day, everything seems less –
your husband's loyalty, the childhood of your child. But the gardenias –
their leather, their scent, the way they take in the light.
You water and cut. Now you remember, now you forget your pain.

Middle-aged and still learning how to measure pain.
On the darker days, you don't bother with your eyes,
or lipstick. There are things you hate: the television light
in the evening, the news, the hours. And in the marriage again,
when you have time (the more of it you longed for), you want less.
You're afraid of staring into the beauty of the gardenias.

You rearrange furniture, you're good at less
clutter. That L-shaped closet you had made, what a pain –
didn't fit through the door. The men stood next to the gardenias
on the balcony, lifted the thing with rope in front of your eyes.
You watched it being pulled upwards like a drunken angel, and again,
the tears, and your throat, and you turned away from the light.

You place the T-shirts in the new closet: here, the light,
here, the dark. Always best to separate. Always less
space than you thought. Some days you dance again,
jump on the bed, make love, make lies, make pain
look beautiful like in the movies, or the thirsty eyes
of teenagers. But always, those goddamn gardenias.

For two nights you hear noises from the gardenias.
You get out of bed, turn on the light,
rub the nightmares from your eyes
and listen – an almost-chirping sound, less

sharp now that a car passes below, headlights like the pain
behind your forehead. You water the plant with whiskey again

and go to bed. But at dawn, the sounds rise – again,
calling you, it seems, from the heart of the gardenias.
So you dig with hands, with nails, with pain,
and see, there near the roots, baby mice, their skin a light
pink, their ears – where are their ears? Less
like mice, more womb-things with under-skin eyes,

blind. Whiskey again. When there's more light
outside, you push the pot out on the street. The gardenias – less
delicate, more painful, more little animals, more almost-eyes.

She Means It

Near the oven, Mom holds
my dad's rifle in his face,

says she's had enough, not anymore, all this
food he keeps bringing into her kitchen:

the fish that need gutting – their eyes;
the crabs that need boiling – their smell;

the bouquets, the bouquets
of parsley – the hands

that chop, the days; all this
bread who needs it

white brown corn *saj* does he
have to try everything? All this

meat, this goddamn meat,
she yells, her freezer's full,

no more room, no more.
She opens it, shows him

the ice has started to melt –
underneath, her heart.

She grabs it, places it back
into her chest, announces

she's leaving, this time
she means it.

Shoulders

Khadijah always burnt the onions, arrived late,
blamed it on the faraway village, the buses.
My mother yelled at her so loud
the entire street heard:

You do this on purpose.
Her neck muscles tightened.
Don't come back on Thursday.
Her veins bulged.
Why do I pay you?
Her face turned red.
*There are many others
in the city. My husband is in love
with himself, and so is my father.*

Then she lit a cigarette and Khadijah got the oil,
pressed her fingers into Mom's shoulders, tried
to loosen the lumps. My mother burped.
Khadijah told again the story of the almonds
her husband brought the day he asked for
her hand in marriage. How he gave her his coat
to hang by the door, screamed at her
for not searching its pockets for her gift,
shook his head, called her stupid.

When I ask what her husband does,
she says, *Tarek? Oh he's a – what do you call it –
pilot.* The women laugh and laugh and laugh.
Khadijah folds a paper into a fan
to cool my mother. When I ask her
about the scarf on her head,
she says, *This? Just a way to keep
the hair out of my eyes, get on with the work.*

Why I Hate Silent Movies

I hate the heat because it reminds me
of the first time he slapped my face.
We were sitting on the sofa and he said
he did it because it was too hot outside.
Later he cried and kissed my feet,
said he would never. I hate flowers
because after he punched me
he got me ice and five bouquets: roses,
lilies, carnations, tulips, and freesias.
I hate jewelry because he bought me
a diamond necklace when he took me out
of the hospital, said *Love me love me love me.*
I hate silent movies because they resemble
my pain back then – all glare and no sound.
I hate bird cages because no matter
how many times I opened them,
the canaries wouldn't fly.
I hate nests because even years after I left
on that day when he strangled the birds,
my hands sometimes smell of feathers
and I still pull out straw, twigs,
and his voice from my hair.

Recipes

The night before I left, you wrote me recipes,
said, *God help us, you don't even know
how to cook rice*, then smiled and added,
Good for you. All night you wrote
about lentils, eggplants, yogurt, peas,
included notes like, *Don't daydream,
remember the fire / Watch out
for the steam as you lift the lid /
Don't burn your eyelashes when you look
into the oven.* An airplane and a few weeks
later, I went through your notes and found
a little prayer. *I hope,*
it read, *I hope you'll forgive
the mistakes I've made.* I knew

what you meant – those afternoons
you pulled at your hair, lay crying
on the bed, told me, *Even Allah
can't stand you right now.* How you chased me
around the house, waved your slipper, flung it
like a boomerang. That time you slapped me
across the face, then walked barefoot
down the building stairs. The days you said,
*I don't want to hear you say the word
mama anymore. Ever.*

So I called you, said things like
hi like *the weather* like *my hips*
are getting wider by the second.
I told you I had managed to cook
your *moujaddara*; you laughed,
said you had no doubt. Then I asked
if you remembered the times

I kept jumping from the top of the closet
unto the bed; how I was convinced I flew, if only
for a few seconds, and how you believed,
said *Yes* said *Good job* said *I see you.*

Mother, Ka'aba

I moan and the nurse reminds me, *The Prophet said heaven is under the feet of mothers.*

When mothers give birth, the heaven under their feet is dark. The first milk, called colostrum, isn't white, she explains, places the pump on my breast.

*

Your mother then your mother then your mother then your father, said the Prophet, says the nurse. She insists I change the feminine pads regularly. Warm baths help.

*

The blood, the days – they don't stop. The pads irritate me. My husband gives me his white cotton undershirts to cut and use instead. Each shirt, a small offering. Each shirt, as white as milk, then dark.

*

The nurse tells me she missed her prayer rug after her first delivery. *Because we can't pray until the bleeding stops.* She peels the tape off my skin to remove the IV. She says mothers, too, are a kind of *Qiblah*, the direction in which we all pray in the end.

She presses her thumb into my arm. Mothers, a kind of *Ka'aba*. Removes the catheter. Final pilgrimage back to where we came from. Alcohol pad, gauze. Mothers, a first temple. Give thanks, circle seven times, counterclockwise. *Mabrook*, she smiles, *what a beautiful baby girl.*

Milk

I couldn't give you my uterus
for more than eight months,
so I wanted to make sure I could
at least give you milk.
Only one breast swelled and filled,
so my friends said *Let it be, let it
go*. But I timed myself, pumped milk
every four hours, even at night,
as if you were there, waking me, as if
you weren't in a hospital incubator.
The noise of the pump
broke the night silence, its rhythm
like a heartbeat – clenching, releasing.
I placed the liquid in freezer bags, wrote
dates on them. The nurses were shocked
so much milk could come out of just
one breast. I thought it was darker
than I expected, and denser.
When we brought you home, swaddled and tiny,
my family finally dared to laugh
at me, walking around with one breast
bigger than the other. I told them I liked
the fullness of it, and love
was always asymmetrical.

Room 607

By then the doctors had removed the tubes
that came out of your lung; by then your fever
had dropped and you were eating again; by then
the cafeteria chef would recognize my voice
on the phone, ask if you were having your usual,
rice with *laban*; by then the woman next door had
died, her family had prayed; by then the old man at the end
of the hall had stopped shouting, *I'm blind! I'm blind!*
all night; by then you were sitting in your hospital bed
smiling, offering me coffee from a pink plastic cup;
by then the nurses knew the name of the two-year-old
with severe pneumonia, and knew her mother,
the one who'd slept with her in the ICU, the one who ran
down the corridor as the nurse tried to find her daughter's
vein again; by then we had filled your room
with toys, books, crayons, because parents want
to make their children feel like children
everywhere – in hospitals, in refugee tents, in shelters;
by then we were already preparing for that ride back
home, when you pointed, *Mom! Dad! Look!
A beautiful tree!* and so were the cars, the street,
the traffic lights and the sky, which was finally vaster
than a window frame for the first time in six weeks.

The Invented Mothers

There are mothers made out of yellow daisies
blooming near a grave. In Palestine,
a little girl presses her ear against her mother's
tombstone, as if to listen – *yalla tnam, yalla tnam*,
the lullabies of the dead are the most beautiful.
Striped school uniform, pink backpack,
blue wristwatch to keep the time,
for even after the dead, there are things to learn,
like reading, and maps, and minus one.

There are mothers made out of chalk.
In Iraq, a little girl sleeps inside
a drawing of her mother on the concrete,
the parent's dress like a boat
big enough for her to sail in. For now,
even this waterless womb would do.
The child's thick black hair spills
on the floor, which is her mother's chest,
and somewhere, even after the cemeteries,
the trees put on their almond-flower dresses.

Fatimah (The Mother Of Her Father)

I told myself the past would be darker than the future.
All mothers do this. That is why endless churches
are named after Maryam. What words now, what incantation?

Pray for the child fed the words of Allah and forced
to carry a gun.
Pray for the infant born in the tent
and the breasts wept dry.
Pray for the daughters who become the mothers
of their fathers and long to be dust.

My right hand, its wound-eye open,
still hangs from necks, says, Stop

wishing pregnant women boys.
Wasn't it boys who murdered mine,
boys who slaughter boys every day
in deserts, in cities, in offices,
with sword, with horse, with bomb,
with black flag, with money?

Look around you – every city, Karbala.
No water in the sea – only wailing.
Some days, I want to spit in the faces of men.

Consider the belly button, the umbilical cord,
what the womb once gave you –
that is how you inherit pain. Beware. It is not
only your body you carry.

What hymn now, what healing?

Have mercy on God, who is your mother,
and weeps and weeps and weeps for you.

Say Love Say God

I liked the idea of an impossible love.
I was told a love so different can't
make children with souls
worth praying for. But those stories
in the Bible and the Qur'an,
love, we knew what they meant.
When you said *sin*, love, you did not
mean my legs, or the way
you were already inside me.
When you said *sin*, you meant
how one forgets. Do you remember
how we slept naked? You were there.

I believed love is immortal, irrational,
and sometimes, tired. The sun, it seems, worships only
the bodies of the young. When I say *old*,
I mean how far we've traveled, love, how we go
back. When I walk new cities, I always
think of you, love. I tell you, *Look* –
lives upon lives upon lives.
Sometimes heaven is when I'm away from you, love.
Sometimes heaven is only the two of us. I know you
understand. Only petty loves want to be worshipped.

I liked the idea of an impossible god.
I was told a god so different can't
make children with souls
worth praying for. But those stories
in the Bible and the Qur'an,
god, we knew what they meant.
When you said *sin*, god, you did not
mean my legs, or the way

you were already inside me.
When you said *sin*, you meant
how one forgets. Do you remember
how we slept naked? You were there.

I believed god is immortal, irrational,
and sometimes, tired. The sun, it seems, worships only
the bodies of the young. When I say *old*,
I mean how far we've traveled, god, how we go
back. When I walk new cities, I always
think of you, god. I tell you, *Look* –
lives upon lives upon lives.
Sometimes heaven is when I'm away from you, god.
Sometimes heaven is only the two of us. I know you
understand. Only petty gods want to be worshipped.

There Was and How Much There Was

There was and how much there was.
Women gather in this living room.
They empty and fill the coffee cups.

> I count the flowers on the curtains
> when we... I get bored.

> Try oil. I like the glide
> of our bodies in the night.

> My friend's mother showed her
> a video about it, the week before
> she got married. I was still single,
> and I asked. No one would tell.

The women laugh.
The walls don't have ears here.
Everybody is a woman here.
Some women bleed. Some don't.

> Did you?

> Every woman bleeds
> one way or another.
> I wear fewer clothes, less
> hair on my body, and still
> he doesn't. Where can I find
> the sugar?

There was and how much there was.
All the women here love chocolate.

>   My first husband, he wanted me
>   to hide my arms, my legs, my laughter.
>   I told myself love means to change –
>   bullshit. I knew how much he loved
>   his money, so I flung his wallet
>   from the balcony. It opened its leather
>   wings and fell flat onto the street.
>   I told him I did it
>   because I hate long skirts.
>   I made sure my second husband
>   likes to drink and dance and carry me
>   on his shoulders in the middle of the club.

The woman in the blue dress starts singing.
The others clap, sway
their heads, their shoulders.
Ya salaam, Allah, Allah.

>   When I was a little girl, my mother
>   told me I was beautiful, but not as much
>   as her. I took her kohl pencil and drew
>   a mole on my left cheek. All I wanted
>   were lips, eyes, hair, hips, a smile
>   like Hind Rostom.

The women sigh.
Ah, Hind Rostom.
They have all seen *La Anam*.

>   I heard she refused a million
>   *gineih* offer to turn her life
>   into a drama series.
>   Oh what I wouldn't give.
>   Some bitch at the gym today
>   walks in, stands in front of me,

talks to my husband. Size 36 women
get away with everything.
Hind Rostom wasn't a size 36.
I shouldn't, really,
but pass the chocolate.

There was and how much there was.
One woman switches on the TV.
It's time for her Arabic-translated
Mexican show. Last episode.
Antonio is about to kill his brother
and marry Rachel.

    Have you heard about Marwa?
    Her husband took a second wife.
    She keeps quiet because of the money.
    The other day, I asked the sheikh
    about Aisha, the prophet's wife.
    I said, "Is it true she was often jealous
    and once told him this God of his
    only brings down *ayahs* convenient?"

One woman says she read that
somewhere. Or heard it.
Says marriage will make you say
strange things. Faith too.

    The sheikh spent half an hour telling me
    a story about honey and the Prophet's wives.
    I forget what it was. When I kept asking,
    he reminded me it was the rasool
    we were talking about. I said, "But
    wasn't he mortal?
    And if he bathed too long
    wouldn't the tips of his fingers
    have shriveled up, like ours would?"

The women agree but advise her
to ask for forgiveness, nevertheless.

استغفر االله

Antonio has killed his brother.
Gun still in hand, he kisses Rachel.
The women change the channel.
There's an old Egyptian play.

> Oh keep that one. It cracks me up.
> This is Raya, this is Sakina.
> They are sisters who kill
> women and steal their jewelry.
> In the end, one kills her daughter
> without knowing it. Once she knows,
> the play turns tragic. My favorite kind.
> You laugh so much and in the end
> you cry and think where
> did this come from.

There was and how much there was.
One woman says she always cries
when she watches a movie on the airplane.

> It's so embarrassing but yes,
> every single time. Like when Diane Lane
> cheated on Richard Gere and I'm thinking,
> why am I crying? What's that got to do
> with me?

The women pass the nuts, the cheese.
Some drink orange juice, some wine.

My fifteen-year-old son lectured me
about the wine the other day.
He said it was *haram*.
He asked why I've not gone
to Mecca with his father last year.
I said, "You know what
Allah says? He says,
Respect your mother."
I told him, "YOU came out
of ME. Shut up." I told him
all religion is metaphor.
He asked what's metaphor.

The women's laughter is louder.
One woman says no man
understands metaphor.

    Pass me that bottle, I need
    another drink. Sometimes I feel
    I should've aimed better
    when I flung my slipper at him
    when he was a child. Should've
    hit that head of his, knocked
    the stupid out of it.

There was and how much there was.
The woman with the black fringe
knows how to read the coffee cups.
The women say, "Please, please."

    I see a big white fish. It means
    money. I see a narrow wavy road.
    It means sickness, or perhaps
    bad news. This is the head of a bird
    here, its small beak. Perhaps you

have a burden; it will be lifted,
inshallah. Children are good,
snakes are bad. You will travel.
Lick your thumb and press it
against the bottom of the cup.
I hope your print is white
like the sun. But don't listen
to me. This is just for fun.
Allah says fortune tellers lie,
even when they tell the truth.

The women light their cigarettes.
The men are playing cards somewhere,
the children are sleeping.

    Last week, at the mall,
    I was peeing and I heard
    a woman tell her friend
    her hair was falling out.
    I started crying. My hair,
    it's falling out too. I keep
    a picture in my bag
    of my graduation night.
    Look, look how pretty
    I was, how tiny my waist.

The women look. They tell her
she is beautiful. Her daughter
looks just like her, *smallah*.

    My daughter fights with me
    all the time. Nothing I do
    makes her happy.
    The other day I told her,
    "You cow." I felt bad

       five minutes later,
       made myself some coffee.
       I try to tell my husband,
       but he blames me.
       I prefer to mumble it all
       to the kettle as it boils.

The women nod.
They yawn, they stretch.

       Look how late it's getting.
       This talking never ends.
       We better leave before
       your husband comes back home.
       See you next week.

There was and how much there was.
Before they leave, the women
wrap the leftover cake
with aluminum foil.
They throw out the cigarettes, the ash.
They collect the empty glasses.

Notes:

p.1:
"There was and how much there was" is a literal translation of كان يا ما كان, which is how traditional Arabic tales start. It is usually translated as "Once upon a time."

p.3: "Layla"
Layla is the lover of Qays Bin Al Mulawwah, 7th century Arab poet. He is known "Majnun Layla," which is Arabic for "crazy about Layla." The story is that Qays Bin Al-Mulawwah fell in love with Layla, but her father didn't allow them to get married. He is said to have lost his mind and exiled himself into the wilderness, where he spent his time composing love poems for her.

p.17: "The Invented Mothers"
Yalla Tnam is the title of a traditional Arabic lullaby. It translates as "Come on, sleep."

p.18: "Fatimah (the Mother of her Father)"
Fatimah is prophet Mohammad's daughter, and it is only through her that his lineage was preserved. She was known as "the mother of her father."

p.21-25: "There Was and How Much There Was"
Hind Rostom was a famous Egyptian actress, known as the Marilyn Monroe of Egypt. *La Anam* is the title of one of her movies, and it translates as "I Don't Sleep."

An ayah is a verse of the Qur'an. استغفر الله is a common expression used to ask God for forgiveness. Translates as "God forgive."

30 years
of smith|doorstop poets

Moniza Alvi, David Annwn, Simon Armitage, Jane Aspinall, Ann Atkinson, David Attwooll, Anne-Marie Austin, Sally Baker, Mike Barlow, Kate Bass, Paul Batchelor, Suzanne Batty, Zeina Hashem Beck, Chris Beckett, Peter Bennet, Catherine Benson, Gerard Benson, Paul Bentley, Sujata Bhatt, David Borrott, Nina Boyd, Maxwell Boyle, Sue Boyle, Carol Brierly, Susan Bright, Carole Bromley, Sue Butler, Peter Carpenter, James Caruth, Liz Cashdan, Dennis Casling, Julia Casterton, Claire Chapman, Debjani Chatterjee, Linda Chase, Geraldine Clarkson, Stephanie Conn, Stanley Cook, Bob Cooper, Jennifer Copley, Julia Copus, Rosaleen Croghan, Tim Cumming, Paula Cunningham, Simon Currie, Duncan Curry, Ann Dancy, Emma Danes, Peter Daniels, Peter Daniels Luczinski, Joyce Darke, Jonathan Davidson, Kwame Dawes, Owen Davis, Julia Deakin, Nichola Deane, Steve Dearden, Patricia Debney, Mike DiPlacido, Maura Dooley, Tim Dooley, Jane Draycott, Basil du Toit, Christy Ducker, Carol Ann Duffy, Sue Dymoke, Stephen Duncan, Suzannah Evans, Michael Farley, Rebecca Farmer, Nell Farrell, Catherine Fisher, Janet Fisher, Anna Fissler, Andrew Forster, Katherine Frost, Sam Gardiner, Adele Gèras, Sally Goldsmith, Yvonne Green, David Grubb, Harry Guest, Robert Hamberger, David Harmer, Sophie Hannah, John Harvey, Jo Haslam, Geoff Hattersley, Jeanette Hattersley, Selima Hill, John Hilton, Andrea Holland, Holly Hopkins, Sian Hughes, Keith Jafrate, Lesley Jefferies, Chris Jones, Mimi Khalvati, John Killick, Jenny King, Mary King, Stephen Knight, Judith Lal, John Lancaster, Peter Lane, Michael Laskey, Kim Lasky, Brenda Lealman, Tim Liardet, Katherine Lightfoot, Semyon Izrailevich Lipkin, John Lyons, Maitreyabandhu, Paul Matthews, Eleanor Maxted, John McAuliffe, Michael McCarthy, Rachel McCarthy, Patrick McGuinness, Kath McKay, Paul McLoughlin, Hugh McMillan, Ian McMillan, Allison McVety, Julie Mellor, Hilary Menos, Paul Mills, Hubert Moore, Kim Moore, David Morley, Sarah Morris, Blake Morrison, Paul Munden, Daljit Nagra, Dorothy Nimmo, Stephanie Norgate, Christopher North, Carita Nystrom, Sean O'Brien, Padraig O'Morain, Mark Pajak, Nigel Pantling, Alan Payne, Pascale Petit, Stuart Pickford, Ann Pilling, Jim Pollard, Wayne Price, Simon Rae, Irene Rawnsley, Ed Reiss, Neil Roberts, Marlynn Rosario, Padraig Rooney, Jane Routh, Peter Sansom, Tom Sastry, Michael Schmidt, Myra Schneider, Rosie Shepperd, Lemn Sissay, Felicity Skelton, Catherine Smith, Elspeth Smith, Joan Jobe Smith, Cherry Smyth, Martin Stannard, Pauline Stainer, Paul Stephenson, Mandy Sutter, Matthew Sweeney, Diana Syder, David Tait, Pam Thompson, Dennis Travis, Susan Utting, Stephen Waling, Martin Wiley, Tony Williams, Ben Wilkinson, Andrew Wilson, David Wilson, River Wolton, Sue Wood, Anna Woodford, Cliff Yates, Luke Samuel Yates

Laureate's Choice 2015 pamphlets
still available from the Poetry Business

David Borrott | Nichola Deane | Rachel McCarthy | Wayne Price

This is a varied but coherent collection, tender, imaginative and clear-eyed. – Carol Ann Duffy

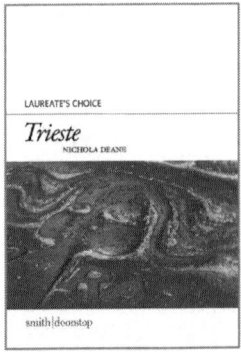

A poet both sophisticated and lyrically charged who deploys imagery that is both precise and daring. – Carol Ann Duffy

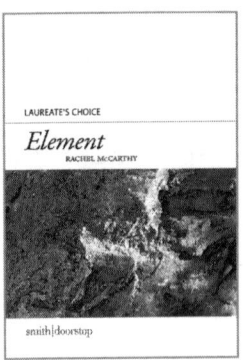

Here are bold poems in a collection that is much more than the sum of its mesmerising parts.
– Carol Ann Duffy

A remarkable new poet who is intelligent, insightful, imaginative and utterly assured.
– Carol Ann Duffy

£7.50 each or all 4 for £20

www.poetrybusiness.co.uk

Thirty poems to celebrate thirty years of Poetry Business pamphlets

Founded in 1986 on an Enterprise Allowance, the Poetry Business was based for twenty years in a Victorian Arcade in Huddersfield, with poets Peter Sansom and Janet Fisher as co-directors. After Janet's retirement, the poet Ann Sansom took over as co-director and the business moved to its present offices in Bank Street Arts in Sheffield.

For all of those 30 years, we have been publishing pamphlets of one shape or another, starting with Simon Armitage's first published poems in *Human Geography*, right up until the present day with our Laureate's Choice pamphlets by four up-and-coming poets chosen by Carol Ann Duffy.

30 at thirty brings you thirty poems, one from each of the thirty years of the Poetry Business.

£5

www.poetrybusiness.co.uk